For my sister, Katy, and brother, Derek
AA

To our grandmother Zhou Jinhua, who inspired
our more than forty-five-year artistic career.
And to our mother and father, who gave us life,
faith, and wisdom.
SZ and DZ

Special thanks to Amy Alznauer for her talent and sensitivity
in condensing the story of our lifelong pursuit of art into a
touching story for children. —SZ and DZ

First edition 2020

Library of Congress Catalog Card Number pending
ISBN 978-1-5362-0428-5

20 21 22 23 24 25 TWP 10 9 8 7 6 5 4 3 2 1

Printed in Johor Bahru, Malaysia

This book was typeset in Adobe Jenson Pro.
The illustrations were done in ink and watercolor.

Candlewick Press
99 Dover Street
Somerville, Massachusetts 02144

www.candlewick.com

Flying Paintings

The Zhou Brothers:
A Story of Revolution and Art

Amy Alznauer

paintings by

ShanZuo Zhou and DaHuang Zhou

CANDLEWICK PRESS

At first there was only one brother.
He was not even a brother yet, just Shaoli,
born in the back of a bookstore on the
highest hill in Wuming, China.

All around him books lay quietly on the tables, and out the window, mountains waited by the water.

His grandmother, Po Po, told him stories of paintings that once flew through the air and still lived on those mountain cliffs. She also told stories of violence. "Bandits and then soldiers destroyed this store," she said. "Twice I built it up again."

The world is a beautiful and terrible place, thought Shaoli.

Soon another boy, Shaoning, arrived. He cried in his mother's arms so long and hard that Shaoli had to cover his ears and hide.

A brother, too, is a beautiful and terrible thing, he thought.

But now he was not alone. In no time two brothers raced in the garden with slingshots and bare feet. Two brothers sat together looking out the window or learning to copy bamboo and plum blossoms with brushes and ink.

Shaoli loved to watch petals from one book float through his brush and bloom again on a blank page.

He also loved to kick Shaoning, sitting so close. And Shaoning loved to kick back.

"To become an artist," Po Po told them, "you must possess the highest spirit."

But the new People's Republic of China did not appreciate the high spirits of people who ran their own stores and made their own art. They threw the brothers' father into labor camp and, later, their mother into prison. They came and burned all the books, turning the words and paintings to ash.

Even art, thought Shaoli in tears, *is beautiful and terrible.*

Po Po finally closed the bookstore and moved the family into a hut near Daming Mountain. Soon Shaoli was sent to work on the mountain itself.

Again, Shaoli was only one brother.

Up on the mountain, he carried heavy loads with a pole balanced on his shoulders. Once, cutting firewood, he fell from the top of a pine and almost died. Yet he was allowed to paint—always the face of Chairman Mao, but at least he was painting.

He thought of little Shaoning down in the village, hunting for bottles for recycling money, practicing calligraphy on paper scraps.

How Shaoli longed to sit with him by the smoke and light of a cooking fire and listen to Po Po's stories.

"Once there was an artist," he could almost hear her saying, "who saw an Immortal stepping down from the sky. The Immortal said, 'If you paint for one hundred days, I will make your paintings live.'

The artist worked and worked, and then one day the door opened. Images flew off his canvas and danced across the river onto the Huashan cliffs."

Shaoli dreamed of making his own paintings that would fly free.

Four years passed. Beloved Po Po died.

Finally there were two brothers again.
Together they went to find the old bookstore.

With the attic gone and paint peeling, the bookstore
seemed to be weeping for Po Po. In sorrow, Shaoli
began to sketch. Shaoning sketched too. Soon flowers
bloomed on the blank walls.

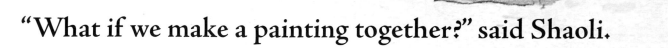

"What if we make a painting together?" said Shaoli.

He sketched the crest of a wave. Shaoning took his brush and changed how the water swelled.

"How dare you destroy my work?" Shaoli said.

But then he looked. The painting was better now.

Side by side they worked, like two little boys again, painting and fighting. Finally they stood back to see what they had made. Two figures riding in a little boat on crashing waves.

"It is like the world and like our lives," said Shaoning.

"Yes," said Shaoli. "Terrible and beautiful."

If together with their brushes they could sail out on a stormy sea or turn a sad house into a garden, they had to keep painting. But how? The government didn't approve of art like theirs, which put them in danger.

Po Po's voice came to them: *"To become an artist, you must possess the highest spirit."*

They applied to school after school. Finally an art school in Shanghai accepted Shaoli but not Shaoning.

Shaoli sent art supplies home. Shaoning sent letters back. "What is left for me is only loneliness," he wrote.

Then one day there was a knock at Shaoli's door. It was Shaoning!

Now two brothers acted as a single artist. By day Shaoli attended classes. By night Shaoning snuck into the studio and drew the required figures until dawn.

But it was not enough. They wanted to be free, to paint not what they were supposed to paint but what they felt.

Yet when school ended, they still had no money, no place to work, and no idea how to capture that wild feeling in their own art.

Again Po Po came to them: "*Once an artist saw an Immortal stepping down from the sky . . .*"

Yes! They would return home and go see the cliff paintings.

Perched in a rowboat or up on a bamboo ladder, they spent days copying the ancient figures. Some looked joyful, dancing and drumming, and some angry, holding knives.

Living on raw fish and wild plants, they sketched and sketched until the images entered their dreams and mixed with their own joy and anger. And their dreams grew until they seemed to catch up everything—the little bookstore, Po Po, their lost family, and all the years of toil and hope.

In a frenzy to paint their dreams, the brothers found a dusty warehouse and worked in secret day and night, always side by side on the same canvas.

Sometimes they were joyful, moving as if part of the same body. Sometimes they waged a little war.

"You have ruined my work!" cried Shaoli.

"No, you have destroyed everything!" cried Shaoning.

But always they found a way to go on together.

Around this time, China was changing. The government began to celebrate not just paintings of Chairman Mao but ancient Chinese art and modern art from Europe and America.

So when Shaoli and Shaoning finally opened the warehouse door,
it was as if the wild images came to life and flew out into the world.

Each canvas was a battle of paint that transformed what was once two into a single dance, what was old into something new, and what was terrible into something beautiful.

Today, the Zhou Brothers are world-renowned artists. They work together in a brick studio in Bridgeport, Chicago. Often it reminds them of the bookstore that once stood on the highest hill in Wuming. Inside, paintings hang quietly on the walls. Outside, instead of mountains, buildings fill the sky. And here, too, sometimes violence flares. But often, people walk inside and study their paintings so long and hard that the images lift off the canvases and enter their own dreams.

AUTHOR'S NOTE

A besieged family, a wise old grandmother, a country in the midst of revolution, and two young brothers with a single, impossible, wild dream. These sound like the ingredients of a great legend, some long-ago adventure that we only hope might be true. But sometimes legends come to life, and sometimes actual lives turn into legend.

"Doubters in the future may question whether [the Zhou Brothers] ever really existed," a *New York Times* journalist wrote. "They did. They do. They flourish."

The Zhou Brothers, who as children went by the names Shaoli and Shaoning, are indeed real, as real as you and me. They were born in the 1950s, during the early days of the People's Republic of China, and came of age during the Cultural Revolution. In some ways they were unlucky. Their family owned a bookstore. And the government did not approve of private business. This led to all sorts of misery—their father taken just before Shaoning was born, their mother taken later, a sister sold away, poverty, hard labor, and a disgraced family name.

But by the same token, they were also lucky. Their family owned a bookstore. And bookstores are amazing things, full of ideas and beauty. And this bookstore was special, for in it lived a grandmother who opened up the books and showed the little brothers the magnificent world within.

So from the beginning the brothers learned the lesson that great legends teach: the very thing you love the most often brings the most trouble. This mix of love and trouble gave birth to a dream. The brothers would take their difficult life and find a way to transform it into something beautiful, a dream they realized by painting together on the same canvas.

Painting together is difficult for the brothers. As difficult as loving their homeland, China, even when it has caused them great trouble. As difficult as loving each other, even when they fight. But painting together is worth the difficulty. "When you paint by yourself, you won't have the courage to destroy your own painting," says DaHuang (the name Shaoning goes by now). "You think you are always right. But two people together, they don't care. With this kind of fighting something comes out that's never happened before. It creates a new magic."

The story I tell here is the legendary bones of their lives that brought forth this new magic. To create the story, I left out many things. For example, the younger brother, Shaoning, was actually born in the village of Ningming, not Wuming, but still in the province of Guangxi and actually closer to the location of the Huashan cliff paintings. There were three other siblings. And there were many Chinese artists and friends who helped the brothers along the way.

After the brothers opened the doors of their dusty warehouse, they still had a great adventure before them. They left promising art careers in China to take a big risk. They packed up their paintings in suitcases and came to America with nothing—no money and no place to live—to start all over again. And once again from nothing they rose to fame. In 2011, US president Barack Obama commissioned a painting from the Zhou Brothers and eventually presented it as a gift to Chinese president Hu Jintao.

Today, the brothers, who now go by ShanZuo and DaHuang, run the Zhou B Center in Bridgeport, Chicago, and are opening new art centers in Beijing, China, and Kansas City, Missouri. Both centers encourage and support new artists, giving them space to work and an audience. The brothers hope to share their story to give other artists, even very young ones, the courage to struggle through their own mix of love and trouble until a new magic is born.

ShanZuo and DaHuang Zhou standing in front of the
Huashan Mountains, where the cliff paintings still dwell

PHOTOGRAPH © 2019 BY ERIN ZHOUSHI